EXTRAORDINARY
FAITH
STUDY GUIDE

EXTRAORDINARY
FAITH
STUDY GUIDE

SHEILA WALSH

NELSON REFERENCE & ELECTRONIC
A Division of Thomas Nelson Publishers
Since 1798
www.thomasnelson.com

Published by Thomas Nelson, Inc., P.O. Box 141000, Nashville, Tennessee, 37214.

Scripture quotations are taken from *The Holy Bible*, New King James Version (NKJV). Copyright © 1979, 1980, 1982, 1992 by Thomas Nelson, Inc. Used by permission. All rights reserved.

Scriptures quotations marked NCV are taken from *The Holy Bible*, New Century Version ®, copyright © 1987, 1988, 1991 by Word Publishing, a division of Thomas Nelson, Inc. Used by Permission.

Scripture quotations marked NLT are taken from *The Holy Bible*, New Living Translation, copyright © 1996. Used by permission of Tyndale House Publishers, Inc., Wheaton, Illinois 60189. All rights reserved.

Scripture quotations marked MSG are taken from *The Message*. Copyright © by Eugene H. Peterson 1993, 1994, 1995. Used by permission of NavPress Publishing Group.

Scripture quotations marked AMP are taken from the Amplified® Bible, Copyright © 1954, 1958, 1962, 1964, 1965, 1987 by The Lockman Foundation. Used by permission. (www.Lockman.org)

Scripture quotations marked PHILLIPS are taken from Copyright © J.B.PHILLIPS 1958, 1960, 1972. THE GOSPELS © Macmillian Publishing Company, a division of Macmillian, Inc. 1952, 1957. THE YOUNG CHURCH IN ACTION © Macmillian Publishing Company, a division on Macmillian, Inc. 1955. LETTERS TO YOUNG CHURCHES © Macmillian Publishing Company, a division of Macmillian, Inc. 1947, 1957. THE BOOK OF REVELATION © Macmillian Publishing Company, a division of Macmillian, Inc. 1957.

Published in association with Yates & Yates LLP, Literary Agents, Orange, California.

Library of Congress Cataloging-in-Publication Data is available.

ISBN 0-7852-5264-9

Printed in United States.

HB 11.30.2023

TABLE OF CONTENTS

INTRODUCTION

∞

If you were asked to define faith, I wonder what would come to mind. I've heard the word used in many different contexts.

"O ye of little faith!"

"Where is your faith?"

"Keep the faith!"

"I've got the faith for it!"

"She's a real woman of faith!"

"Great is Thy faithfulness!"

"God is faithful, and He will do it!"

Faith can be defined as confidence, trust, assurance, conviction, and belief. Webster defines faith as "belief and trust in and loyalty to God." Through this study we'll look at God's track record of faithfulness, the power of a mustard seed faith, and the unexpected value of doubt in strengthening our faith. We'll learn that faith means trusting that God is in control, even when our faith is put to the test. We are women who are walking by faith until we see our Savior's face. My prayer for us as we travel through these pages together is that God, by His Holy Spirit, will give us a fresh understanding of faith—of what it is and what it is not.

LESSON I

FAITH DEFINED

∞

Faith means being sure of the things we hope for and knowing that something is real even if we do not see it."

—Hebrews 11:1 NCV

"*N*ow faith is the substance of things hoped for, the evidence of things not seen" (Heb. 11:1 NKJV). Throughout the whole canon of Scripture, we have the preceding fifteen words offered to us as the only definition of faith. In other passages we have pictures of those who exhibited faith, what it looks like to break faith, constant exhortations to have faith or stand firm in the faith, to live by faith, rebukes of those with little faith, those who are rewarded because of their faith, and those who will turn away from their faith. But Hebrews 11:1 is the only actual definition of what the content of faith looks like.

1. Indeed, no other verse in Scripture says, "Faith is…." But we can round out our understanding of faith by comparing other passages. Where does Romans 10:17 say our faith comes from?

_____

_____

_____

_____

_____

_____

2. What does Romans 5:2 say we have access into because of our faith?

_____

_____

_____

_____

_____

_____

_____

3. According to Galatians 3:26, who have we become because of faith in Jesus?

_____

_____

_____

_____

_____

_____

4. Take a look at these passages. They help us to understand what faith is and what it can accomplish in our lives. Match up each statement with the verse in which it is found.

_____ Acts 6:5   a. The church can be strengthened in the faith.

_____ Acts 15:9   b. We have boldness and confidence through faith.

_____ Acts 16:5   c. Hearts are purified by faith.

_____ Romans 11:20   d. We are kept by God through faith.

____ Ephesians 3:12   e. You can stand by faith.

____ Ephesians 3:17   f. Believers can be full of faith.

____ 1 Peter 1:5   g. Christ dwells in our hearts through faith.

"Faith has substance to it, and the kind of evidence that demands personal conviction."

Each of these verses gives us a facet of what faith is by giving us a glimpse of faith in action. When the writer to the Hebrews offered his definition, he presented it to us as a present reality, not a pursued reality. By that I mean he wrote assuming that the reader already has faith. There is great significance in that. Faith is something to be experienced and exercised, not defined, categorized, and neatly packaged.

EXTRAORDINARY FAITH STUDY GUIDE

5. Faith can seem so insubstantial, and yet it is the very thing believers stand upon. Faith means being sure, certain, convinced. How does Proverbs 3:26 put faith into words?

"For the _____ will be your _____" (NKJV)

6. That sounds so positive, so simple. But the psalmist reminds us that we are apt to place our confidence in the things we can see and hear and touch. What contrast do we find in Psalm 118:8–9?

_____

_____

_____

_____

_____

_____

_____

We often call this faith in the unseen "blind faith," or we'll say we're taking a leap of faith. But Hebrews 11 assures us that faith has real substance to it. But what we are called to is not blind and stupid adherence to something that makes no sense. The Greek word used for "substance" in Hebrews 11:1 is *hupostasis*. It is a scientific term that means actual, physical evidence as opposed to theory or hypothesis. And the word used for "evidence" is *elegchos*. It is a rock-solid legal term. It is a strong, inclusive term in Greek, meaning the kind of evidence that will be accepted for conviction.

Faith has substance to it, and the kind of evidence that demands personal conviction.

LESSON I: FAITH DEFINED

7. Faith rests on a solid foundation. The evidence is everywhere before our eyes. God is able to persuade our hearts and our minds to put our trust in Him. When we find faith, it's as if we echo Paul's familiar words, "I am persuaded." What does Paul say he knows in 2 Timothy 1:12, and of what does Paul say he is persuaded?

_____

_____

_____

_____

_____

8. There are other verses that speak of this persuasion as well. They speak of the evidence of something that is unseen, but of which we can be sure.

- What did Paul say he'd seen ample evidence of in Timothy's life, according to 2 Timothy 1:5?

_____

_____

_____

- Of what was Paul persuaded, according to Romans 8:38–39?

_____

_____

_____

9. All this persuasion makes us more confident in our faith. What does 1 John 5:14 say we can be confident about?

_____

_____

_____

_____

_____

_____

10. What else can we be confident about, according to Philippians 1:6?

_____

_____

_____

_____

_____

When we study faith in the biblical context, it has both an active and a passive sense. In an active sense, faith is our loyalty and devotion to God; in a passive sense, our resting confidence in God, in His Word, and in His promises. Faith is not just what we believe, our doctrine or denominational creed, but also and more importantly, a rock-solid conviction that what we believe and whom we believe in are worth staking our lives on; they are real and living.

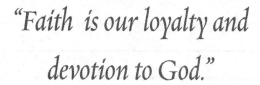

"Faith is our loyalty and devotion to God."

11. In Colossians 2:2, Paul prays that the hearts of believers will be encouraged. One of the encouragements he mentions is "the full assurance of understanding." Here's how this passage looks in a few different translations.

- "Attaining to all the riches of the full assurance of understanding" (NKJV)

- "I want them to have full confidence because they have complete understanding" (NLT).

- "That they may come to have all the abounding wealth and blessings of assured conviction of understanding" (AMP)

- "How I long for you to grow more certain in your knowledge and more sure in your grasp of God himself. May your spiritual experience become richer as you see more and more fully" (PHILLIPS).

- "In touch with everything there is to know of God. Then you will have minds confident and at rest" (MSG).

Why do understanding and assurance encourage us? Why does Paul compare this confidence to riches?

_____

_____

_____

_____

_____

_____

_____

12. Understanding lends us confidence, and the writer of Hebrews goes on to encourage us to hang onto that certainty. Life has a way of shaking things up, but faith can remain our firm foundation.

> Hebrews 3:6 – "Christ as a Son over His own house, whose house we are
>
> if we _____ _____ the _____ and the rejoicing
>
> of the hope _____ to the end" (NKJV).

> Hebrews 3:14 – "For we have become partakers of Christ if we _____
>
> the beginning of our _____ _____ to the
>
> end" (NKJV).

> Hebrews 10:35 – "Therefore do not _____ _____
>
> your _____, which has great _____ "
>
> (NKJV).

"Faith is certainty!"

Christian faith is more than wishful thinking; it is a certainty, a constant assurance based on God's track record in our lives and the lives of the faithful through the generations. It's my prayer that as we look at faith together, we will come to a crystal clear resting place at the end of our journey that our world, the church, and our own lives are filled with overwhelming evidence of the faithfulness of God.

NOTES

LESSON 2

GOD'S TRACK RECORD

∽

"Your mercy, O LORD, is in the heavens; Your faithfulness reaches to the clouds."

—Psalm 36:5 NKJV

*A*braham. I don't know how familiar you are with his story. Most of us raised in church know the basics. God called Abraham to leave his homeland and go to a place God would show him. He had a son, Isaac, when he was very old, and God told Abraham to offer Isaac as a sacrifice. Abraham was willing, and God spared his son. Abraham became known as the great father of the faith, but there is much more to his story. If we will take a close look at the good and bad choices, the moments of faith and of doubt or disobedience, I believe we will find many lessons for our lives today.

I love the fact that the Genesis account shows the development of Abraham's faith. He started with conditional faith that grew and grew, he fell back again and again, and then he developed mature, rock-solid faith. We can learn a lot about faith when we take a look at God's track record with this one man, both when Abraham displayed a lot of faith and when he did not.

1. God is faithful all the time, and His faithfulness has inspired many a song. Do you recognize the hymn and the praise chorus in each of these verses?

• Psalm 89:1

_____

_____

_____

• Lamentations 3:22–23

_____

_____

_____

2. All of the Bible extols the faithfulness of God. He is always true to Himself and to His Word. Here are some of the passages that describe this divine quality. Match each statement with the verse in which it is found.

____ Deuteronomy 7:9   a. Your faithfulness will be declared before the assembly.

____ Nehemiah 9:33   b. God's faithfulness endures to all generations.

____ Psalm 36:5   c. I will sing of Your faithfulness, O God.

____ Psalm 40:10   d. He is God, the faithful God who keeps His covenant.

____ Psalm 71:22   e. God is faithful.

____ Psalm 89:8   f. God's faithfulness reaches to the clouds.

____ Psalm 92:2   g. God, Your faithfulness surrounds You.

____ Psalm 119:90   h. Though we deal wickedly, God deals
                            faithfully.

____ 1 Corinthians 1:9   i. I will declare Your faithfulness every night.

———— ✑ ————

"God always has a plan."

Abraham was told that he would have a son. All he had to do was wait for God to bring that promise to pass. After all, Abraham knew that God was a faithful God. All he had to do was trust. But he didn't, and that brings up a lot of questions in our minds. If God is so faithful, why didn't Abraham trust Him? Couldn't he have taken the Lord at His word? Why couldn't he have just waited patiently? Why did Abraham try to take matters into his own hands? Did he think God couldn't keep His promises without a little help? Why did Abraham have to make such a mess of things? It's easy to read the Bible through critical eyes and wonder why Abraham made certain choices, but God understood and patiently worked with Abraham.

3. What God is doing doesn't always make sense. Abraham couldn't see God's plan, so he devised one of his own. But Scripture is clear—God always has a plan.

- What does David say about the plans of the Lord in Psalm 33:11?

_____

_____

_____

_____

_____

- What does Proverbs 16:9 remind us about our plans?

_____

_____

_____

- According to Proverbs 19:21, whose counsel should we seek when making our plans?

_____

_____

_____

_____

LESSON 2: GOD'S TRACK RECORD

"God is patient and faithful even when our obedience is limited."

4. What promise can we depend upon, when it comes to God's plans for us? It's found in Jeremiah 29:11.

_____

_____

_____

_____

_____

_____

_____

5. Abraham had to wait for years to see God's promise come to pass. Even when we know that God's timing is the best, the hardest part is the waiting.

- What does David urge his own soul to do in Psalm 62:5?

_____

_____

_____

- What does the psalmist say God will do for those who wait on Him, according to Psalm 27:14?

_____

_____

_____

_____

- What gives us hope while we are waiting, according to Psalm 130:5?

_____

_____

_____

_____

- What is good, according to Lamentations 3:25–26?

_____

_____

_____

_____

"Waiting is hard. We feel as if we are doing nothing, and very often we are tempted to intervene."

6. What is God's promise to those who wait on Him in Isaiah 40:31?

_____

_____

_____

_____

_____

_____

7. Even now, we are waiting for the fulfillment of God's promise.

Romans 8:25 – "If we _____ for what we do not _____,

we eagerly _____ for it with _____" (NKJV).

Galatians 5:5 – "For we through the Spirit _____

_____ for the _____ of righteousness by

_____" (NKJV).

Philippians 3:20 – "For our _____ is in _____,

from which we also _____ _____

for the Savior, the Lord Jesus Christ" (NKJV).

Hebrews 9:28 – "To those who _____ _____

for Him He will _____ a second time, apart from sin,

for salvation" (NKJV).

"Offer your scars to the One who is scarred for you."

And then God told Abraham he'd have to sacrifice his son. Just when Abraham had everything he'd ever wanted, God asked for it all back. But Abraham's faith had changed by this time. His trust in God had grown. Do you see it? Do you see what God had worked in Abraham by then? God had a track record with Abraham. Abraham had blown it over and over again, and yet God had remained faithful.

God had proved Himself to Abraham in such profound ways that Abraham knew Isaac was the boy God promised his descendants would come from. If God said it, God would do it! Abraham knew that even if he had to plunge the knife into his son's heart, God could raise him from the dead.

8. Abraham had seen the impossible come to pass. His own son was evidence of that. And Abraham knew that God had promised that Isaac would be his heir, and that through him Abraham would have more descendants than there were stars in the sky. Though he couldn't see God's plan, Abraham trusted God.

_____	Psalm 32:10	a. Blessed are those who trust in You, O LORD.
_____	Psalm 34:8	b. Those who trust in God will find perfect peace.
_____	Psalm 57:1	c. Mercy shall surround the one who trusts in the LORD.
_____	Psalm 84:12	d. Those who trust in their own heart are foolish.
_____	Proverbs 28:26	e. Blessed is the one who trusts and has their hope in You.
_____	Proverbs 29:25	f. God is good. Blessed are those who trust in Him.
_____	Isaiah 26:3	g. Whoever trusts in the Lord shall be safe.
_____	Jeremiah 17:7	h. My soul trusts in God. He is my refuge.

As a young woman I imagined that living a life of faith meant that I needed to do more, believe more, be more. Would the call to Extraordinary Faith be a clarion call to do more? No, of course not. I think again today of Mary Graham's words to me—"faith is not about us, it's about God's gift to us when we need it most."

9. Faith, like salvation, is a gift from God. How does Paul describe this gift in Ephesians 2:8–9?

_____

_____

_____

_____

_____

_____

10. Fill in the blanks:

Galatians 2:16 – "Knowing that a man is not _____ by the _____ of the law but by _____ in Jesus Christ" (NKJV).

Philippians 3:9 – "And be found in Him, not having _____ _____ righteousness, which is from the law, but that which is through _____ in Christ, the righteousness which is from _____ by _____" (NKJV).

Romans 4:5 – "But to him who does not _____ but

_____ on Him who _____ the ungodly, his

_____ is accounted for righteousness" (NKJV).

Romans 3:28 – "Therefore, we conclude that a man is _____ by

_____ apart from the _____ of the law" (NKJV).

--------- ✑ ---------

"Whatever you are facing right
now, be it the worst of times or
the best, remember you are loved
by a God who spared nothing of
Himself to show His faithfulness."

Over and over God's Word makes it clear that we have no righteousness of our own, yet how often do you and I try to prove to God that we are worthy? I think back to the years I spent working harder and harder in Christian ministry, trying to win God's approval, missing the whole point that God's favor rests on those who come with nothing in their hands and the blood of the Lamb on their hearts.

11. Faith comes by believing—believing that Jesus Christ is the Son of God, and that He died so that our sins could be forgiven. That's why believers say that they're saved by the blood. We come with nothing in our hands and the blood of the Lamb on our hearts.

Romans 5:9 – "Having now been _____ by His

blood, we shall be saved from wrath through Him" (NKJV).

Ephesians 1:7 – "In Him we have _____ through

His blood, the forgiveness of sins, according to the riches of His grace"

(NKJV).

Hebrews 9:14 – "How much more shall the blood of Christ, who through

the eternal Spirit offered Himself without spot to God, _____

your conscience from dead works to serve the living God?" (NKJV).

12. As you look at your life today, with all the pieces that seem to work well and the bits that don't, my prayer is that you will take some time and write out for yourself what God's track record is with you.

_____

_____

_____

_____

_____

_____

_____

_____

God's Word is all about His faithfulness to us even when we are faithless! I am convinced, won over, sure, persuaded, and certain that faith is not about what we are able to muster up; it is indeed all about God's faithfulness revealed through Jesus.

NOTES

_____

_____

_____

_____

_____

_____

_____

_____

_____

_____

_____

_____

_____

_____

_____

_____

_____

_____

_____

_____

_____

_____

_____

_____

_____

_____

_____

LESSON 3

FAITH AS A MUSTARD SEED

"I say to you, if you have faith as a mustard seed, you will say to this mountain, 'Move from here to there,' and it will move; and nothing will be impossible for you"

—Matthew 17:20 NKJV

bout three years ago Nashville was graced with a large outlet mall, Opry Mills. We avoided it for the first few months, as the crowds were overwhelming. But when we did go, one of the first things that Christian saw was a rock-climbing wall inside a sports store. "Can I do it, Mom? Please, please, please!" I read the sheet that parents had to sign relinquishing the store of all responsibility when Christian's rope snapped and he plummeted to the ground, poking his eye out on the way down! Barry signed, and we got in line.

Christian started to climb. At one point he stopped and looked back at us. "I'm doing it! I'm doing it!" he cried. There was such a look of pure, unadulterated joy at his achievement. As he got closer to the top, however, he faltered. He looked for Barry. "I don't think I can go any farther," he said.

"That's cool, Christian. You've done great. Do you want to come down now?" Barry asked.

"I don't really want to, but I'm afraid."

"Then just take one more step," Barry coached.

Christian took one more and stopped. Then he took another. I sat and watched as he calculated each deliberate step. Sometimes he waited for a while, but then he moved again. In just a few moments he was at the top, and he reached out and rang the bell.

Christian's experience that day seemed to me to be a reflection of the Christian life and the place of faith. We start well, we falter, we almost turn around—but we don't want to, for where else would we go? So we take one more step, just one more little step even though the journey is almost too much for us—almost.

1. Often the faith we have seems small—too small. But all we need is the faith to take one more step. What does Luke 17:6 say about small faith?

_____

_____

_____

_____

_____

_____

2. Another mustard seed text is found in Matthew 17:20. What does this verse say we can do with a little faith?

_____

_____

_____

_____

_____

_____

3. A mustard seed is also compared to the kingdom of God in Luke 13:19. When such a seed is planted in our own lives, what does the Lord say becomes of it?

_____

_____

_____

_____

_____

———————— ✌ ————————

"It's not about what we can do. It's about who God is."

The word used for "mustard seed" in the New Testament is the Egyptian word *sinapi*. It refers to a plant that begins as a very tiny seed, but if planted in good, fertile soil, it grows to ten or twelve feet. In Matthew 13 Jesus said that the mustard seed, although it is the least of all seeds, grows above all other herbs and offers shelter for the birds of the air. That's quite a bit of progress from such small beginnings.

Jesus referred to mustard-seed faith twice in the Book of Matthew, once in Mark, and twice in Luke's Gospel. Each instance gives us a different picture of faith. When you look at all the references to mustard-seed faith together, the picture becomes a little clearer. The kingdom, the work of God in our hearts, begins as a small seed, but as it is placed in good soil—the Word of God, prayer, fellowship—it grows and offers shelter to others.

4. Having faith for the impossible isn't easy. Facts, worries, and fears tend to get in the way. In Mark 9:24, we find a man who knew his faith was lacking. What did he ask Jesus for?

_____

_____

_____

_____

_____

_____

_____

5. God helps us when we ask, because He knows just what we need. In fact, one of God's many names is Helper. Match up these verses, which talk about God's helpfulness.

____ Psalm 30:10   a. I will pray and the Father will give you another Helper.

____ Psalm 54:4   b. Jesus sent the Helper to believers.

____ Psalm 86:17   c. The Helper will come from the Father.

____ Psalm 118:13   d. God is my helper.

____ John 14:16   e. The LORD is my helper, I will not fear.

____ John 14:26   f. You, LORD, have helped me and comforted me.

____ John 15:26   g. LORD, be my helper.

____ John 16:7   h. The Helper will teach you all things.

____ Hebrews 13:6   i. You pushed me, but the LORD helped me.

6. God knows we're weak. He knows there are times when our faith falters. But what is His promise to us, according to 2 Corinthians 12:9?

_____

_____

_____

_____

_____

——————— ⸎ ———————

"Whatever you are facing right now, God is with you."

I don't know where you find yourself as you read this book. You may be in a time where life seems to be smooth sailing. You may be facing the kind of circumstances that seem huge until you compare them to the events occurring in someone else's life—then you realize that you have little to complain about. You may be in the worst days of your life right now, crying out, "Where are You, God?" Sometimes in our lives we become so discouraged that we doubt God's care. We find ourselves asking, "God, do You see me? Do You know what I long for, and does that matter to You?"

7. God is gracious to us, even when our faith for the task ahead seems mustard-seed small. But the promise we have is that a mustard seed's worth of faith is all we need. And we have it! Paul tells us so in Romans 12:3.

"God has dealt to each one a _____ of _____"

(NKJV).

8. Of course, we needn't be stranded with a speck of faith for all our lives. What do the apostles ask of the Lord in Luke 17:5?

_____

_____

_____

_____

_____

_____

_____

9. What faith-related item of news does Paul rejoice over in 2 Thessalonians 1:3?

_____

_____

_____

_____

_____

_____

_____

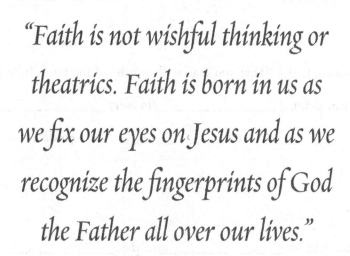

"Faith is not wishful thinking or theatrics. Faith is born in us as we fix our eyes on Jesus and as we recognize the fingerprints of God the Father all over our lives."

10. Faith grows because we're alive. God often speaks of our spiritual lives in such terms—seeds, vines, growth, and fruit. All of us are growing, even in our faith, towards maturity.

Luke 8:15 – "The ones that fell on the good ground are those who, hav-

ing _____ the word with a _____ and good

_____, keep it and _____ _____ with

patience" (NKJV).

John 15:5 – "I am the _____, you are the _____.

He who abides in Me, and I in him, _____ much

_____; for without Me you can do _____" (NKJV).

Colossians 1:10 – "That you may walk worthy of the Lord, fully pleasing Him, being _____ in every _____

_____ and _____ in the knowledge of God" (NKJV).

2 Peter 3:18 – _____ in the _____ and

_____ of our Lord and Savior Jesus Christ (NKJV).

11. Think of times in your own life when God has answered a specific prayer or intervened in a miraculous way. Did that change you, or did it draw you closer to God?

_____

_____

_____

_____

_____

_____

_____

_____

_____

The mustard seed of faith is so small when it's contrasted with the mountains that need moving. As I read and studied, it seemed clear that Jesus used the enormity of a mountain to show how God moves on behalf of His people. I think again of Mary Graham's words that faith is not about our mustering up huge reserves of mountain-moving power but about leaning on Christ, trusting our Father, and taking one more step. We start with what we have.

NOTES

_____

_____

_____

_____

_____

_____

_____

_____

_____

_____

_____

_____

_____

_____

_____

_____

_____

_____

_____

_____

_____

_____

_____

_____

_____

_____

_____

_____

_____

_____

SURPRISED BY DOUBT

*"O my people, trust in him at all times. Pour out
your heart to him, for God is our refuge."*

—Psalm 62:8 NLT

Within the Christian community we seem to put pressure on ourselves and each other to say the right thing rather than the true thing. No one wants to admit that they struggle with doubts, because we aren't supposed to doubt. This is a huge issue for us to address if we want to embrace and live a true and pure faith. I wonder how many people have walked away from a relationship with God because their inner doubts and questions have overwhelmed and isolated them.

As believers we find it easy to share what we perceive to be our great moments of faith or insight, but we usually keep our doubts to ourselves. I want us to look together at the gift that doubting can be to our spiritual lives. That may sound strange, but I believe that doubts, honestly expressed and wrestled with, produce a faith that is stronger and more intimate than doubts suppressed under the veneer of faith.

1. We have doubts, it's true. But we also know that we're not supposed to have doubts. What does Jesus say about doubting—and about not doubting—in Mark 11:23?

_____

_____

_____

2. Remember Doubting Thomas? He's famous for refusing to believe what he could not verify by the evidence of his own eyes (John 20:24–25). When Thomas finally did get the evidence he'd demanded in John 20:29, what did Jesus say?

_____

_____

_____

_____

_____

———————— ✍ ————————

"I encourage you to bring your doubts to Him. He can be trusted with your questions."

3. How is the doubter described in James 1:6?

_____

_____

_____

_____

_____

_____

I find that those who walked with God in the Old Testament seem far more honest than those of us in the church today. The psalmist David was brutally honest with God. The prophets poured out their hearts to God; Job railed against God. Those who were able to bring their doubts and fears, however raw, into the presence of God, and who truly wrestled with their faith, found a faith that could withstand anything. Doubts unexpressed isolate us and drive us from the heart of God. God's heart is big enough to carry whatever burden you are bearing.

4. You have doubts? Tell God about them. Be honest with the Lord, and pour out your heart before Him. He promises to hear you. Match up these verses with the Scripture passage in which they are found.

_____ Psalm 10:17   a. Hear, O LORD, and have mercy on me.

_____ Psalm 17:6   b. Hear me, O LORD, for Your
                             lovingkindness is good.

_____ Psalm 30:10   c. LORD, You have heard the desire of the
                             humble.

_____ Psalm 62:8   d. Pour out your heart like water before
                             the Lord.

_____ Psalm 69:16   e. O God, incline your ear to me and hear.

_____ Lamentations 2:19   f. Trust God. Pour out your heart before
                             Him.

5. Don't hide your doubts. It's silly to try to hide how you feel from the Lord. After all, God knows our hearts better than we do.

- What does David tell Solomon about how well God knows people in 1 Chronicles 28:9?

_____

_____

_____

_____

- What does Solomon then say God knows in 1 Kings 8:39?

_____

_____

_____

_____

- If we were to echo Psalm 139:23, what would our prayer be?

_____

_____

_____

_____

_____

_____

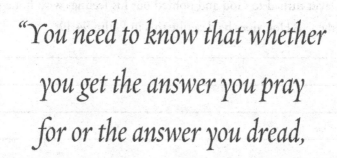

"You need to know that whether you get the answer you pray for or the answer you dread, God's grace will be enough."

6. Trust the One who knows your heart, loves you completely, and wants only the best for you.

Psalm 7:9 – "You _____ _____ within the _____ and _____, O righteous God" (NLT).

Psalm 19:12 – "How can I know all the _____ _____ in my _____? _____ me from these _____ _____" (NLT).

Psalm 44:21 – "God would surely have _____ it, for he _____ the _____ of every _____" (NLT).

Psalm 139:1 – "O LORD, you have _____ my _____

and _____ everything about me" (NLT).

7. When David turned to God and poured out his feelings with honesty, his faith was strengthened. How does he describe this in Psalm 94:19?

_____

_____

_____

_____

_____

_____

_____

_____

_____

Peter illustrates for us all the potential for good, for nobility and courage in a human heart, while modeling also what is flawed and faithless. Remember the storm at sea, and Peter's desire to walk on the water? Jesus said, "Come." So Peter stepped out of the boat and onto the water with the others looking on in amazement. I think it is a gift to us that after walking on the waves for a moment, Peter looked down and began to sink. I receive two things from that illustration: Christ is strong, and I am weak. If I keep my eyes on Jesus, I can walk over troubled seas to Him, but it's not because I've perfected Walking on Water 101. It's only because I am looking at Jesus. It was not that Peter had suddenly become a magician but rather that as long as he kept his eyes on Christ, the impossible became possible.

"Why did you doubt?" (Matt. 14:31). Great question! Not "How could you doubt?" or "I can't believe you doubted!" Jesus simply asked why. There is no condemnation in that question, but a call to Peter to examine his heart.

8. Each of us needs to examine our heart from time to time. God may know just what's going on inside of us, but sometimes we aren't as aware. What does 1 Corinthians 11:28 encourage believers to do?

_____

_____

_____

_____

_____

_____

9. Sometimes this exploration of our hearts is best done in tandem with the Lord. What does David invite the Lord to do in Psalm 26:2?

_____

_____

_____

_____

_____

_____

10. More often than not, when we turn our eyes inward and examine our hearts, the Spirit reveals to us areas of sin that need taking care of. What does Lamentations 3:40 say goes hand in hand with self-examination?

_____

_____

_____

_____

_____

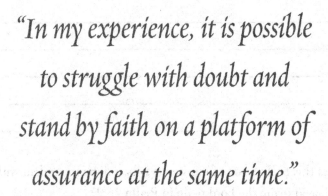

"In my experience, it is possible to struggle with doubt and stand by faith on a platform of assurance at the same time."

Jesus wanted Peter to come to a greater understanding of what it means to walk by faith, not by sight. Asking why of ourselves when we doubt is an important step toward faith. Peter could say that he doubted because he took his eyes off Jesus and looked down—a good lesson for the future, for there were many moments of faith and doubt ahead. One of the most remarkable examples of simple faith came through an unlikely vessel.

11. We, like Peter, want to come to a greater understanding of faith. Our doubts drive us to God for answers. As we examine our hearts with His help, we are changed.

- What is David's prayer along these lines, as found in Psalm 51:10?

_____

_____

_____

_____

- What does David want the Lord to do according to Psalm 51:12?

_____

_____

_____

_____

Peter had to be hauled up out of the water before the wind and the waves buried him. Jesus did not calm the storm that time; He grabbed hold of His friend in the midst of the storm and held him. In my own life, sometimes Jesus has spoken to the stormy circumstances I was in and immediately calmed the sea. Other times, though, even as the storm continued to rage around me, I have cried out to Him and He has reached out and grabbed hold of me. One of my passions as we take this journey of looking at faith together is that we see whether Jesus calms the storm or calms us in the storm, His love is the same, and His grace is enough.

NOTES

LESSON 5

GOD IS IN CONTROL

∞

"Your faith should not be in the wisdom of men but in the power of God."

—1 Corinthians 2:5 NKJV

*F*aith is believing that no matter how things appear on the surface, God is in control. I think that is both faith's challenge and reward. The challenge is that humanly we want to see with our own eyes what God is doing. We are willing to give an unwavering yes to God if we know His plan and are given the opportunity to sign off on it. But the adventure and reward of faith is that He asks us to trust based on who He is, not on what we can see.

If you ever feel overwhelmed by everything that's going on in your world and wonder if things are totally out of control, take heart! I think as we trace God's hand through these lives, we will see clearly that no matter what appears to be true, our God is in control.

1. We don't always understand why God does what He does, but we can rely on the fact that God is in control. Where does Paul say we should (and should not) place our faith, according to 1 Corinthians 2:5?

_____

_____

_____

_____

_____

2. God is in control, and God is quite capable in that role. How does 1 Corinthians 1:20 compare His qualifications to ours.

_____

_____

_____

_____

_____

———— ✑ ————

> *"We don't always see God's plans take place before our eyes. We don't always get to be the ones who marvel at the fulfillment of them all."*

3. Paul calls God, "alone wise" (Rom. 16:27 NKJV). How does Job 9:4 describe the Lord?

_____

_____

_____

_____

_____

4. What contrast does Paul make between God and us in 1 Corinthians 3:19?

_____

_____

_____

_____

_____

I don't always understand why God works as He does, why He heals one and not another, why He delivers one and not another, but I do believe that He is good all the time. Our faith is tested in many ways. Sometimes we are immersed in a situation that seems hopeless, and we wonder, God, are You there? Sometimes He delivers us from a situation in such a miraculous way that we know it had to be God; sometimes He calls us to walk with a limp, following the One who was wounded for us.

I don't know what you have walked through or what pain you have known. I don't know where you find yourself at this moment, but I encourage you to invite Christ into the midst of your struggles and heartache. Offer your scars to the One who is scarred for you. The very wounds that seemed that they might break you will be used by God to strengthen you and to give strength to others.

5. The Lord understands what we cannot. When we are in need, He knows what is needed. What does Psalm 147:5 tell us about the Lord?

_____

_____

_____

_____

_____

6. The path to realizing that indeed our heavenly Father knows best, and being able to rest in that with confidence and joy, is often a painful one.

____ Psalm 5:8	a. Make God's footsteps our pathway.	
____ Psalm 61:2	b. Lead me, LORD. Make Your way straight before me.	
____ Psalm 85:13	c. Your word is a light to my path.	
____ Psalm 119:105	d. When I was overwhelmed, You knew my path.	
____ Psalm 142:3	e. When my heart is overwhelmed, lead me to the rock.	

———— ⁄⁄ ————

"It is a long and twisted road for many who are called to walk in God's shadow."

I remember as a young woman making bold declarations to the Lord: "Lord, I want to be used by You, whatever it takes." "Take my life, Lord, and mold me to be more like Jesus." "Father, I long to be a conduit of Your love." I sincerely meant those prayers. I just had no idea that the path that led to being made more like Christ could be such a dark and lonely place, or that molding requires so much pressure and heat.

7. We're familiar with the chorus, which invites God, "Take me. Mold me. Fill me. Use me." But being the pot means submitting to the Potter and trusting His plans for our use.

Isaiah 29:16 – "Shall the _____ be esteemed as the

_____; For shall the thing _____ say of him

who _____ it, 'He did not _____ me'?

Or shall the thing _____ say of him who _____

it, 'He has no _____'?" (NKJV).

Isaiah 64:8 – "O LORD, You are our Father; We are the _____,

and You our _____; And all we are the _____ of

Your _____" (NKJV).

Romans 9:20–21 – "Indeed, O man, who are you to reply against God?

Will the thing _____ say to him who _____ it,

'_____ have you _____ me like this?' Does not

the _____ have _____ over the _____"

(NKJV).

8. When we are willing to let God have control—admitting that He's the Potter and we are His to use—what kind of vessel does 2 Timothy 2:21 say that we can become?

_____

_____

_____

_____

9. God does not always tell us why His plans are different from our plans; He just asks us to trust Him. Remember Joseph? Do you think he understood God's foresight while he was being sold into slavery, accused of attempted rape, and sentenced to prison? No. But Joseph trusted, and in hindsight, what does Genesis 50:20 tell us he was able to say?

_____

_____

_____

_____

_____

God's faithfulness to this boy was easier for him to see in retrospect than when he was living through long years of betrayal, false accusations, and imprisonment. That may be true for you, too. Again, we don't always get to see God's plan when we are living in it. Afterwards, Joseph was able to recognize the intricacies of God's planning. He told his brothers that he knew their intentions, but God was bigger than any of their plans. Joseph was able to trace the hand of God.

10. What is the promise that so many believers cling to—in Romans 8:28 (NKJV)?

And we _____ (with confidence, by faith)

That _____ _____ (the good, the bad,

and the ugly)

Work together for _____ (even if it doesn't make sense

to us at the time)

To those who _____ God (trusting Him with their

whole heart)

To those who are _____ (God's choice for the task at

hand)

According to _____ _____ (not our

own preferences).

As a young believer I wanted to think that if God was with me, He would protect me from the harsher experiences in life, but that is not the promise here. The promise is that wherever the path takes us, God will be there.

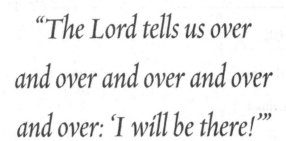

"The Lord tells us over and over and over and over and over: 'I will be there!'"

11. In the end, having the faith to believe that God is in control means trusting God no matter what. Other things have their allure, and beckon us to put our trust in them instead, but they always fail eventually.

- What worldly signs of wealth and security called to David's heart according to Psalm 20:7?

_____

_____

_____

_____

- What does Psalm 118:8 say we shouldn't put our confidence in?

_____

_____

_____

_____

• According to Proverbs 28:26, what are we foolish to trust?

_____

_____

_____

_____

12. God alone is completely faithful and worthy of our trust. If He says all things will work together for good—His good—we can believe it.

• Why does Psalm 9:10 say we can trust God?

_____

_____

_____

_____

• Why does Psalm 18:2 say we can trust God?

_____

_____

_____

_____

• Why does Psalm 115:11 say we can trust God?

_____

_____

_____

_____

"Now faith is the substance of things hoped for, the evidence of things not seen" (Heb. 11:1 NKJV). This opening definition is a challenge to those of us who like rules and regulations, clear direction and control, and a call to get over ourselves! Faith requires great trust and rock-solid belief in the promises of God. Following Christ is a direct call to let go of our human need to understand everything and trust God.

NOTES

NOTES

LESSON 6

PUT TO THE TEST

∽

"The LORD tests the righteous."

—Psalm 11:5 NKJV

*M*y friend Janice battles against cancer, yet her faith is unshaken. I am humbled by the faith of my friend. I am humbled by her vulnerability. I am humbled by her honest expression of grief and struggle and fear and yet the clear song of faith that she sings through it all. It's a different song from what I once imagined. It's not a song that tells us that if we just have enough faith, everything in our lives will be smooth and easy. At times this new song is in a minor key, and the notes seem lonely and bleak; but the song of faith is one that tells all that is true within the context of the greatness of God.

David's psalms often have the same bittersweet quality. Within the same song David cries out about what is true and harsh, and yet he reaffirms his faith in God, who hears him and loves him. At times theologians have struggled with David's brutal honesty. Some prayer books have performed psalmectomies—editing out the most raw emotion as if to protect us. That seems wrong to me unless they can also protect us from the realities of life. We need the companionship of other honest souls who have wrestled with their faith and said out loud what is rumbling around in their souls.

1. David and Job were both famous for questioning God. They weren't afraid to ask God, "Why?" Match up these pointed questions with the verse in which they're found.

____ Job 7:20   a. Why is there so much war?

____ Job 9:29   b. Why are You using me for target practice?

____ Psalm 2:1   c. Why do You seem so far away just when I
                        need You most?

____ Psalm 10:1   d. Why have You forsaken me?

____ Psalm 22:1   e. Why do I have to do all this pointless work?

God is not offended by our honest questions, for they are a hallmark of a true relationship. When our faith is tested, we have questions. And when we wrestle with the answers to our questions, our faith is strengthened.

2. What does Jeremiah 17:10 say that the Lord does?

_____

_____

_____

_____

3. Why does Deuteronomy 13:3 say that God tests His people?

_____

_____

_____

_____

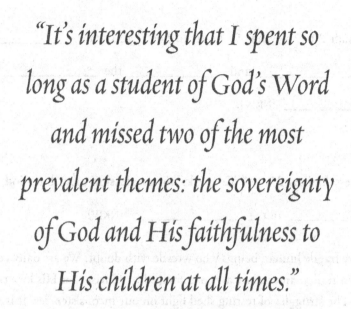

"It's interesting that I spent so long as a student of God's Word and missed two of the most prevalent themes: the sovereignty of God and His faithfulness to His children at all times."

4. God tests the hearts of His people—Scripture is clear on that point. In doing so, He uncovers our true feelings, our level of commitment, and our willingness to walk by faith.

1 Chronicles 29:17 – "I know also, my God, that You _____

the _____ and have _____ in _____"

(NKJV).

Psalm 7:9 – "The righteous God _____ the _____

and _____" (NKJV).

69

Psalm 11:5 – "The LORD _____ the _____"

(NKJV).

Jeremiah 20:12 – "But, O LORD of hosts, You who _____

the _____, and _____ the _____ and

_____" (NKJV).

1 Thessalonians 2:4 – "We speak, not as pleasing men, but God who

_____ our _____" (NKJV).

We are fragile human beings who wrestle with doubt. We are daily confronted by our own frailty, and yet we are so embraced by Christ that His love transforms our lives. The struggles of testing shed light on our inconsistencies. It is one thing to think that you are doing everything right and that is why God is smiling on you, but it is a life-transforming moment when, just as you realize you have got it all wrong, Christ receives you anyhow.

5. What does Proverbs 17:3 say this testing process is like?

_____

_____

_____

_____

_____

_____

_____

6. The refining process removes the dross, or impurities, from metal. But in order for the precious materials to be made pure, they must be subjected to intense heat. Compare these descriptions as you fill in the blanks.

Zechariah 13:9 – "I will bring the one-third through the _____,

will _____ them as _____ is _____,

and _____ them as _____ is _____"

(NKJV).

Malachi 3:2–3 – "But who can endure the day of His coming? And who

can stand when He appears? For He is like a _____

_____ and like _____ _____. He will

sit as a _____ and a _____ of _____;

He will _____ the sons of Levi, and _____ them

as _____ and _____" (NKJV).

Psalm 66:10 – "For You, O God, have _____ us; You have

_____ us as _____ is _____" (NKJV).

1 Corinthians 3:13 – "Each one's work will become clear; for the Day will

declare it, because it will be _____ by _____; and

the _____ will _____ each one's work, of what sort

it is" (NKJV).

7. The testing process is not easy. Our struggles may seem like the melting heat of a fiery furnace. But we can be assured that the process will be worthwhile. What does Job 23:10 say will happen once the testing is over?

_____

_____

_____

_____

_____

8. James makes a similar observance in the New Testament. What does he tell us about the results of testing in James 1:2–4?

_____

_____

_____

_____

In this context James was addressing those who were facing trials and struggles at every turn. His encouragement was to ask God for wisdom. "Help me see Your hand in this, Father." "Give me the strength to go through this, Father." "Show me which way to turn." These are the prayers of God's beloved children going through difficult times. James encourages us to ask God to show us how He is working a bad situation for good.

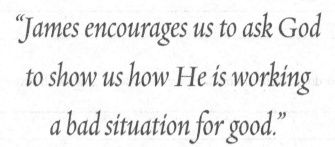

"James encourages us to ask God to show us how He is working a bad situation for good."

9. What was Peter's prayer for believers, according to 1 Peter 1:7?

_____

_____

_____

_____

_____

_____

_____

God tests us to see if we love Him with our whole heart. He tests us to see if our faith will prove genuine. He tests us so that we will grow and change and understand and mature. Through testing, we become stronger, more useful vessels in His hands.

10. The testing process builds trust as it deepens our dependency on God. It's a relationship builder. Trials and testing aren't supposed to drive us from God or make us resentful. They should cause us to seek Him out all the more.

- What does Deuteronomy 4:29 urge us to do with all our heart?

_____

_____

_____

_____

- What does Deuteronomy 6:5 urge us to do with all our heart?

_____

_____

_____

11. We've already considered the faith of Abraham in this study. Here was a man who learned to trust God in the face of the impossible. What do later accounts of Abraham's life tell us about this man of faith?

- What is Abraham called in 2 Chronicles 20:7?

_____

_____

_____

_____

- How does James describe Abraham in James 2:23?

_____

_____

_____

_____

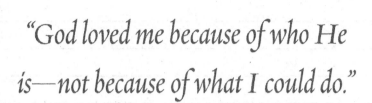

"God loved me because of who He is—not because of what I could do."

12. What did Jesus say to His followers in John 15:15?

_____

_____

_____

_____

_____

_____

_____

_____

One day on the beach, as I sat looking out at the sea and praying, I heard God talk to me. It was not an audible voice but an unmistakable one, and what He said to me was so simple but so profound. "I have many servants and few friends; many who will do things for Me, few who just want to love Me. Sheila, I don't want your work; I want your heart." That encounter transformed me. Many life-altering moments lay ahead, but I knew on that day, sitting on a rock carved out by the sea and the waves, that God loved me because of who He is—not because of what I could do.

NOTES

_____

_____

_____

_____

_____

_____

_____

_____

_____

_____

_____

_____

_____

_____

_____

_____

_____

_____

_____

_____

_____

LESSON 7

WALKING BY FAITH

∽

Opening Scripture Verse: "Walk in the steps of the faith which our father Abraham had."

—Romans 4:12 NKJV

*H*ebrews 11 is often called the Hall of Faith. In it we find the great "cloud of witnesses"—men and women who followed God faithfully. The first of these faithful ones mentioned is Abel. "By faith Abel offered to God a more excellent sacrifice than Cain, through which he obtained witness that he was righteous, God testifying of his gifts; and through it he being dead still speaks" (Heb. 11:4 NKJV). Abel didn't rely on his own efforts or ingenuity. Abel asked God what He wanted, and brought an acceptable sacrifice. Abel's legacy to us is simple but profound. His life shows us that God looks for obedience and an absolute confidence in nothing but the shed blood of Christ.

What does it mean to walk by faith? As I've studied and prayed, I've become convinced that it means that every time my will crosses God's will, I drag my will back in line with His. It means doing the things that I know are good and true, whether I feel like it or not. It means setting my face and heart toward heaven just as Jesus did. I believe that it means that we study how Jesus lived, how He loved, and follow His example. When we find ourselves in a difficult place, we do what He did: we turn to our Father.

1. In the Bible, "walk" refers to our way of life, our lifestyle. So a walk of faith is a lifestyle based upon faith in God. Without that basis, our walk would be little more than hopeless wandering.

- How does Isaiah 53:6 describe us?

_____

_____

_____

_____

- In Jeremiah 18:12, how have the people decided to walk?

_____

_____

_____

- What contrast in walks does Micah 4:5 highlight?

_____

_____

_____

_____

2. One of the earliest commands given to God's people involved walking.

"And now, Israel, what does the LORD your God _____ of

you, but to _____ the LORD your God, to _____

in all His _____ and to _____ Him, to

_____ the LORD your God with all your _____ and

with all your _____, and to _____ the command-

ments of the LORD and His statutes which I command you today for your

_____?" (Deut. 10:12–13 NKJV)

3. The theme of walking in God's ways continues throughout Scripture. Here is a sampling of these Scriptures. Match them with their texts.

_____ Genesis 17:1   a. When you walk through the fire, you shall
                           not be burned.

_____ Exodus 16:4   b. Your servants walk before You with all their
                           hearts.

_____ Exodus 18:20   c. "I am Almighty God; walk before Me and be
                           blameless."

_____ 1 Kings 8:23   d. Walk as children of light.

_____ Psalm 23:4   e. We do not walk according to the flesh.

_____ Isaiah 43:2   f. Show them the way in which they must walk.

_____ Romans 8:1   g. I will not walk in fear of evil because You are
                           with me.

_____ Ephesians 5:8   h. I will test the people, to see if they will walk
                           in My way.

"Perhaps that is the whole point of faith: that we follow God faithfully when nothing makes sense anymore."

4. For better or for worse, each of us *has* a walk. But the question remains—*how* shall we walk? Each of these passages gives us some idea of the how in the adverb it attaches to walk. Write down that word or phrase for each of these verses.

Proverbs 2:7 – Walk _____

Micah 6:8 – Walk _____

Acts 21:24 – Walk _____

Romans 6:4 – Walk ____ _____ ____ _____

Romans 13:13 – Walk _____

Galatians 5:25 – Walk _____ _____ _____

Ephesians 5:15 – Walk _____

Abraham was transformed by his walk with God. He went from a faltering and flawed beginning to an abiding trust in God. In many ways, Abraham had not changed. He was still the same man with the same personality traits, likes, and dislikes. But he had walked with God for so long and watched Him do such amazing things that finally he expected God to show up faithfully, whether it was in ways he could anticipate or in unexpected ways. He knew God would always be there.

5. And there is yet another facet of our walk with the Lord. Where should we be walking, according to each of these verses?

Psalm 26:11 – Walk in _____

Psalm 86:11 – Walk in _____

Psalm 89:15 – Walk in _____

Psalm 119:1 – Walk in _____

Proverbs 2:20 – Walk in _____

John 8:12 – Walk in _____

Ephesians 5:2 – Walk in _____

Colossians 2:6 – Walk in _____

1 John 1:7 – Walk in _____

6. If there is any doubt, what does 1 John 2:6 say is our guideline for walking?

_____

_____

_____

_____

_____

_____

It's not always easy to live a godly life. We think it's only in our generation that society and culture have become so godless, but it has always been a narrow and difficult road for those who want to follow the heart of God.

"I pray that we will receive a clearer picture of what it means to walk by faith, no matter what sight tells us."

7. What is the promise to those who walk uprightly, according to Psalm 84:11?

_____

_____

_____

_____

_____

I'm almost sure that those who make up this great cloud of witnesses had no sense that they were part of such a demonstration of God's grace and faithfulness expressed through human lives. They lived and made choices, not knowing how their lives would encourage us through the centuries.

8. Paul's message about the Christian walk is consistently simple. He says, "You are a Christian. You bear the name of Christ. Walk worthy of the name you bear."

Ephesians 4:1 – "I, therefore, the prisoner of the Lord, beseech you to

_____ _____ of the _____ with which

you were _____" (NKJV).

Colossians 1:10 – "That you may _____ _____ of

the Lord, _____ _____ Him, being

_____ in every good work and _____ in the knowl-

edge of God" (NKJV).

1 Thessalonians 2:12 – "That you would _____ _____

of God who _____ you into His own kingdom and glory"

(NKJV).

9. What does Hebrews 11:6 tell us about the essential nature of our faith?

_____

_____

_____

_____

_____

_____

_____

We read that "without faith it is impossible to please God" (Heb. 11:6 NKJV). God does not want us to die on the altar of our own efforts to please Him. He wants us to come to Him in simple faith through Christ. Take a walk with God every day. You never know where you might end up!

10. With all these things to keep in mind, what should our prayer be, according to Psalm 143:8?

_____

_____

_____

_____

_____

_____

11. Sometimes we are plagued with uncertainties, and wonder which way to turn. What promise do we find in Isaiah 30:21?

_____

_____

_____

_____

_____

_____

_____

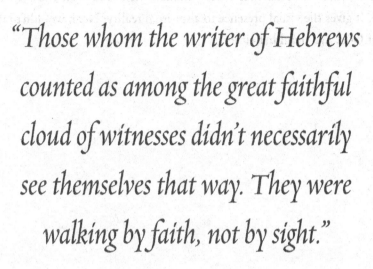

"Those whom the writer of Hebrews counted as among the great faithful cloud of witnesses didn't necessarily see themselves that way. They were walking by faith, not by sight."

12. Each of us has a different set of circumstances. Not one of us is just the same as the woman next to us. But we are all following the same Lord. We are all walking in the same direction by faith. What does Paul urge each one of us to do, according to 1 Corinthians 7:17?

_____

_____

_____

_____

_____

_____

Noah is the first man in Scripture to be called "righteous." He earned this title because his faith in God never wavered. He trusted God even though he had no idea what the outcome would be. When I reflect on his life, I am convinced that Noah must have walked with God many days. It is only when you spend so much time in God's presence that you become convinced of His absolute trustworthiness, no matter what. We read that Noah "walked with God" (Gen. 6:9). I love that picture. It gives the visual presence to a spiritual reality: Noah wouldn't take a step without God. We shouldn't either.

NOTES

NOTES

LESSON 8

UNTIL WE SEE HIS FACE

∽

"Now the just shall live by faith; But if anyone draws back, my soul has no pleasure in him."

—Hebrews 10:38 NKJV

I always thought I had just two options in my life: 1) I could live with full abandon and passion, pour out my life and heart to God and to others, take risks, and give generously of heart and spirit. If I did that, I set myself up for disappointment and loss, for heartache and rejection. 2) I could live cautiously, care about others but not too much, love what I do but not too much, give what I have but hold back some reserve. If I did this I would feel safe; not so alive, but safe.

For years I chose option 2, and I think part of me despised that. As believers we are not called to live safe, small lives. We are called to live as Christ lived, to love as He loves. But here is the dilemma: we can live that way only by faith!

1. We cannot live cautiously, safely, hesitantly. Faith requires us to step out, leap off, and lean on God and His promises. This is our spiritual life, and it cannot be satisfied with temporal things. How does Deuteronomy 8:3 put this into words?

_____

_____

_____

_____

_____

_____

2. How then, are we called to live, according to Romans 1:17?

_____

_____

_____

_____

_____

_____

----------- ✑ -----------

"Extraordinary faith comes from being in relationship with our extraordinary God. It's not about us; it's all about Him."

3. For now we live by faith, and we will continue to live by faith until the day when we see our Lord face to face. In Him, our real life is hidden.

Acts 17:28 – "For in Him we live and move and have our being" (NKJV).

1 Corinthians 8:6 – "For us there is one God...and one Lord Jesus Christ, through whom are all things, and through whom we live" (NKJV).

Galatians 2:20 – "I have been crucified with Christ; it is no longer I who live, but Christ lives in me; and the life which I now live in the flesh I live by faith in the Son of God, who loved me and gave Himself for me" (NKJV).

Colossians 3:3 – "Your life is hidden with Christ in God" (NKJV).

1 John 4:9 – "In this the love of God was manifested toward us, that God has sent His only begotten Son into the world, that we might live through Him" (NKJV).

One of the things I have come to understand about my relationship with God is that I don't always get to feel His presence. I don't get to see the blueprints for my life; I am called to walk by faith. As a young woman, I wanted what many of us want: clear direction at every turn. I wanted to know that God saw me. If I could just tune in to His Spirit, I would never take a wrong turn. The trouble with that belief is that it placed so much importance on me, on my being able to get it all right.

4. Living by faith means realizing that we're not the focal point anymore. It's not up to us to get it all right. Instead, we trust God for what is ahead. Instead of our priorities, we look for God's priorities. What does 2 Corinthians 5:15 say we should live for?

_____

_____

_____

_____

_____

_____

5. What a before and after picture! This is a startling shift for our hearts to undergo. Setting self-interest aside, we now live for God, not for ourselves.

- What contrast does Paul set up for us in Romans 8:5?

  _____

  _____

  _____

  _____

- According to 1 Peter 2:24, what do we now live for?

  _____

  _____

  _____

  _____

- What does Peter go on to tell us we should live for in 1 Peter 4:2?

  _____

  _____

  _____

6. Living isn't just about eating, sleeping, working, and breathing. That's just sur-viving. Jesus invites us to live richly, fully—abundantly.

"I have _____ that they may have _____, and that

they may have it _____ _____"

(John 10:10 NKJV).

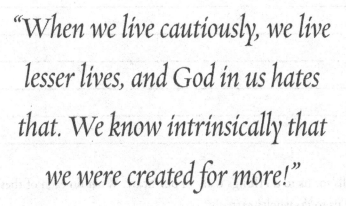

"When we live cautiously, we live lesser lives, and God in us hates that. We know intrinsically that we were created for more!"

7. Living cautiously, safely was like living a half-life. My spirit knew that I had been made for more. God doesn't call us only to have us come halfway. What was Jesus' response to half-hearted people in Revelation 3:16?

_____

_____

_____

_____

_____

8. The life of faith is a whole-hearted affair. Abundant life is there if we will place ourselves incautiously into the hands of God. Take a look at The Message's paraphrase of these familiar words of Christ:

So love the Lord God with all your passion and prayer and intelligence and energy (Mark 12:30 MSG).

Would you say your walk with the Lord is characterized by this description?

_____

_____

_____

_____

_____

_____

_____

_____

9. God calls for us to do things with all our heart. What do each of these passages command us to do wholeheartedly?

Deuteronomy 4:29 – _____ the Lord with all your heart.

Deuteronomy 6:5 – _____ the Lord with all your heart.

Deuteronomy 10:12 – _____ the Lord with all your heart.

Deuteronomy 30:2 – _____ to the Lord with all your heart.

Deuteronomy 30:10 – _____ to the Lord with all your heart.

Proverbs 3:5 – _____ in the Lord with all your heart.

Jeremiah 29:13 – _____ for the Lord with all your heart.

Zephaniah 3:14 – _____ in the Lord with all your heart.

Acts 8:37 – _____ in the Lord with all your heart.

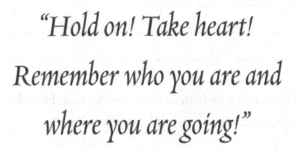

"Hold on! Take heart! Remember who you are and where you are going!"

10. Living abundantly by faith means living wholeheartedly before the Lord. So the only question that remains is, "How long?"

- When does David say he will be satisfied, according to Psalm 17:5?

_____

_____

_____

_____

- What does Job 33:26 say will bring joy?

_____

_____

_____

_____

- What does Paul say he understands now…and then, according to 1 Corinthians 13:12?

_____

_____

_____

_____

11. And so we wait, living by faith until we see His face. How does each of the following verses characterize our lives while we are waiting?

- Colossians 1:23

_____

_____

_____

- Colossians 2:5

_____

_____

_____

- Hebrews 6:11

_____

_____

_____

12. And lastly, what is the culmination of all our faith. Or as it is put in 1 Peter 1:9, what is the end of our faith?

_____

_____

_____

_____

_____

_____

_____

_____

_____

When we have walked through devastating times and found God to be our Rock and Strength in the midst of it all, we are changed. God hasn't changed; we have. He has always been that strong, that loving, that merciful, that present for us, but we never availed ourselves of all of who He is before. Wherever you are in life, no matter what is going on, whether you are in the best days or the worst days of your life, God loves you and will faithfully walk with you through it all.

Let us fix our eyes on Jesus, the author and perfecter of our faith, who for the joy set before him endured the cross, scorning its shame, and sat down at the right hand of the throne of God. Consider him who endured such opposition from sinful men, so that you will not grow weary and lose heart (Hebrews 12:2–3 NIV).

NOTES

_____

_____

_____

_____

_____

_____

_____

_____

_____

_____

_____

_____

_____

_____

_____

_____

_____

_____

_____

_____

_____

_____

LEADER'S GUIDE

∽

LESSON I

1. "So then faith comes by hearing, and hearing by the word of God" (Rom. 10:17 NKJV). Our faith is in God because of what we know of Him from Scripture. Because we had ears to hear the Word, we believe.

2. "Through whom also we have access by faith into this grace in which we stand, and rejoice in hope of the glory of God" (Rom. 5:2 NKJV). Because we have faith, we have found grace, and by the grace of God, we have hope.

3. "For you are all sons of God through faith in Christ Jesus" (Gal. 3:26 NKJV). Not only do we find hope and grace through faith. Through faith, we are adopted into God's own family. He calls us His own. We become sons and daughters of God.

4. <u>f</u> , <u>c</u> , <u>a</u> , <u>e</u> , <u>b</u> , <u>g</u> , <u>d</u>

5. "For the LORD will be your <u>confidence</u>" (Prov. 3:26 NKJV).

6. "It is better to trust in the LORD than to put confidence in man. It is better to trust in the LORD than to put confidence in princes" (Ps. 118:8–9 NKJV). There will be times when we must consciously choose to trust God, even when the world says it doesn't make sense.

7. "I know whom I have believed and am persuaded that He is able to keep what I have committed to Him until that Day" (2 Tim. 1:12 NKJV). Paul says he *knows* the One he believes in. Then he continues by saying he is persuaded that God is able to keep the things Paul has committed into His hands. Paul, nearing his death, is telling Timothy that he is sure—beyond any shadow of a doubt—that Jesus is Lord and that God will keep His promises to those who have put their faith in Him.

8. "When I call to remembrance the genuine faith that is in you, which dwelt first in your grandmother Lois and your mother Eunice, and I am persuaded is in you also" (2 Tim. 1:5 NKJV). We cannot *see* faith in someone's heart, but we can see the evidence of it in the way they live their lives. Paul saw the evidence of faith in Timothy, and was persuaded that it was genuine. "For I am persuaded that neither death nor life, nor angels nor principalities nor powers, nor things present nor things to come, nor height nor depth, nor any other created thing, shall be able to separate us from the love of God which is in Christ Jesus our Lord" (Rom. 8:38–39 NKJV). It's as if the evidence of God's love is so overwhelming, that the faithful cannot help but believe.

9. "Now this is the confidence that we have in Him, that if we ask anything according to His will, He hears us" (1 John 5:14 NKJV). We who have faith can have confidence in prayer. We know that God welcomes our prayers and that He always hears us.

10. "Being confident of this very thing, that He who has begun a good work in you will complete it until the day of Jesus Christ" (Phil. 1:6 NKJV). Though we have faith, we are often discouraged by its apparent weakness. Paul encourages believers to take confidence from the fact that Jesus' good work in our lives is not finished. Our faith can and will grow.

11. Faith is often equated with confidence, conviction, assurance, certainty. Paul encourages believers by telling them that as they grow to understand God and Jesus more, their faith will grow. This strength of conviction drives away doubt. This certainty puts a heart at rest. The closer we grow to God, the deeper our confidence in Him becomes. Such a faith is unshakeable. This encourages us, and is truly the riches Paul speaks of.

12. "Christ as a Son over His own house, whose house we are if we **hold fast** the **confidence** and the rejoicing of the hope **firm** to the end" (Heb. 3:6 NKJV). "For we have become partakers of Christ if we **hold** the beginning of our **confidence stead-fast** to the end" (Heb. 3:14 NKJV). Therefore do not **cast away** your **confidence**, which has great **reward**" (Heb. 10:35 NKJV).

LESSON 2

1. "I will sing of the mercies of the LORD forever; With my mouth will I make known Your faithfulness to all generations" (Ps. 89:1 NKJV). "Through the LORD's mercies we are not consumed, because His compassions fail not. They are new every morning; Great is Your faithfulness" (Lam. 3:22–23 NKJV).

2. <u>d</u> , <u>h</u> , <u>f</u> , <u>a</u> , <u>c</u> , <u>g</u> , <u>i</u> , <u>b</u> , <u>e</u>

3. "The counsel of the LORD stands forever, The plans of His heart to all generations" (Ps. 33:11 NKJV). "A man's heart plans his way, But the LORD directs his steps" (Prov. 16:9 NKJV). "There are many plans in a man's heart, nevertheless the LORD's counsel—that will stand" (Prov. 19:21 NKJV).

4. "'For I know the plans I have for you,' says the LORD. 'They are plans for good and not for disaster, to give you a future and a hope'" (Jer. 29:11 NLT). Even though

we may not understand or even see God's plan for us, we can trust that He has one
and that it is for good.

5. "My soul, wait silently for God alone, for my expectation is from Him" (Ps. 62:5
NKJV). It's as if David is reminding himself to wait and to wait silently. Perhaps he's
trying to calm his own heart by reminding himself that what he's expecting can
only come from God's hand. "Wait on the LORD; be of good courage, and He shall
strengthen your heart; wait, I say, on the LORD!" (Ps. 27:14 NKJV). While we wait
for God, we can take courage from the fact that He is strengthening our heart for
the duration of our waiting period. "I wait for the LORD, my soul waits, and in His
word I do hope" (Ps. 130:5 NKJV). We can take hope—encouragement even—by
clinging to the promises in God's Word. Reminding ourselves that what He has
said will come to pass may help ease the restlessness of waiting. "The LORD is good
to those who wait for Him, to the soul who seeks Him. It is good that one should
hope and wait quietly for the salvation of the LORD" (Lam. 3:25–26 NKJV). Surpris-
ingly, Scripture tells us that it is good to wait—and wait quietly no less! Waiting
patiently shows trust.

6. "Those who wait on the LORD shall renew their strength; they shall mount up
with wings like eagles, they shall run and not be weary, they shall walk and not
faint" (Is. 40:31 NKJV). God doesn't just tell us to wait. He helps us to wait. He gives
us the strength we need to await His perfect timing. He promises that we won't
stumble from weariness or faint from weakness. We will soar like eagles!

7. "If we **hope** for what we do not **see**, we eagerly **wait** for it with **perseverance**"
(Rom. 8:25 NKJV). "For we through the Spirit **eagerly wait** for the **hope** of righteousness by **faith**" (Gal. 5:5 NKJV). "For our **citizenship** is in **heaven**, from which
we also **eagerly wait** for the Savior, the Lord Jesus Christ" (Phil. 3:20 NKJV). "To

those who **eagerly wait** for Him He will **appear** a second time, apart from sin, for salvation" (Heb. 9:28 NKJV).

8. <u>c</u> , <u>f</u> , <u>h</u> , <u>a</u> , <u>d</u> , <u>g</u> , <u>b</u> , <u>e</u>

9. "For by grace you have been saved through faith, and that not of yourselves; it is the gift of God, not of works, lest anyone should boast" (Eph. 2:8–9 NKJV). It's not about how hard we work. It's not about what we can do for God. It's not about being more than we are. It's about receiving a gift we didn't deserve when we needed it most.

10. "Knowing that a man is not **justified** by the **works** of the law but by **faith** in Jesus Christ" (Gal. 2:16 NKJV). "And be found in Him, not having **my own** righteousness, which is from the law, but that which is through **faith** in Christ, the righteousness which is from **God** by **faith**" (Phil. 3:9 NKJV). "But to him who does not **work** but **believes** on Him who **justifies** the ungodly, his **faith** is accounted for righteousness" (Rom. 4:5 NKJV). "Therefore, we conclude that a man is **justified** by **faith** apart from the **deeds** of the law" (Rom. 3:28 NKJV).

11. "Having now been **justified** by His blood, we shall be saved from wrath through Him" (Rom. 5:9 NKJV). "In Him we have **redemption** through His blood, the forgiveness of sins, according to the riches of His grace" (Eph. 1:7 NKJV). "How much more shall the blood of Christ, who through the eternal Spirit offered Himself without spot to God, **cleanse** your conscience from dead works to serve the living God?" (Heb. 9:14 NKJV).

12. We all have a story. We can look at our lives and answer two questions: "Where have I been?" and "Where am I going?" Looking back we can see God's hand on

our lives. And the place we are now may well be where God prepares us for what is in His plans for our future.

LESSON 3

1. "If you have faith as a mustard seed, you can say to this mulberry tree, 'Be pulled up by the roots and be planted in the sea,' and it would obey you" (Luke 17:6 NKJV). Even a small step forward in faith can lead to mountain-moving (or in this case, tree-transplanting) miracles.

2. "Because of your unbelief; for assuredly, I say to you, if you have faith as a mustard seed, you will say to this mountain, 'Move from here to there,' and it will move; and nothing will be impossible for you" (Matt. 17:20 NKJV). Through faith, nothing will be impossible.

3. "It is like a mustard seed, which a man took and put in his garden; and it grew and became a large tree, and the birds of the air nested in its branches" (Luke 13:19 NKJV).

4. "The father of the child cried out and said with tears, 'Lord, I believe; help my unbelief'" (Mark 9:24 NKJV). Even in the midst of believing, we can find ourselves struggling with areas of unbelief. When we need more faith, we need only ask for help.

5. _g_ , _d_ , _f_ , _i_ , _a_ , _h_ , _c_ , _b_ , _e_

6. "My grace is sufficient for you, for My strength is made perfect in weakness" (2 Cor. 12:9 NKJV). God's grace will make up for our shortcomings. He can use us

even when we're weak. It's when we're depending on Him that His strength shines through our lives.

7. "God has dealt to each one a **measure** of **faith**" (Rom. 12:3 NKJV).

8. "And the apostles said to the Lord, 'increase our faith'" (Luke 17:5 NKJV). Faith can be increased. It can be strengthened. It can grow!

9. "We are bound to thank God always for you, brethren, as it is fitting, because your faith grows exceedingly" (2 Thess. 1:3 NKJV). Not only can faith grow, it can flourish to the point that, as Paul puts it, it "grows exceedingly."

10. "The ones that fell on the good ground are those who, having **heard** the word with a **noble** and good **heart**, keep it and **bear fruit** with patience" (Luke 8:15 NKJV). "I am the **vine**, you are the **branches**. He who abides in Me, and I in him, **bears** much **fruit**; for without Me you can do **nothing**" (John 15:5 NKJV). "That you may walk worthy of the Lord, fully pleasing Him, being **fruitful** in every **good work** and **increasing** in the knowledge of God" (Col. 1:10 NKJV). **Grow** in the **grace** and **knowledge** of our Lord and Savior Jesus Christ (2 Pet. 3:18 NKJV).

11. When we see God acting on our behalf, even in small ways, the bonds of trust are strengthened. Trust grows. Faith deepens.

LESSON 4

1. "For assuredly, I say to you, whoever says to this mountain, 'Be removed and be cast into the sea,' and does not doubt in his heart, but believes that those things he says will be done, he will have whatever he says" (Mark 11:23 NKJV).

2. "Then Jesus told him, 'You believe because you have seen me. Blessed are those who haven't seen me and believe anyway'" (John 20:29 NLT). Believers today all must have the faith to trust in a Lord they haven't seen. We believe anyway, and Jesus says we're blessed.

3. "He who doubts is like a wave of the sea driven and tossed by the wind" (James 1:6 NKJV). Helplessly driven to and fro. Vacillating with every shift of the wind. If your life is ruled by doubts, you'll never have stability, you'll always be second-guessing yourself, and you'll be plagued by worry.

4. __c__ , __e__ , __a__ , __f__ , __b__ , __d__

5. "For the LORD searches all hearts and understands all the intent of the thoughts" (1 Chr. 28:9 NKJV). God knows our every thought, intention, and ulterior motive. "Give to everyone according to all his ways, whose heart You know (for You alone know the hearts of all the sons of men)" (1 Kin. 8:39 NKJV). None of us can hide what is in our heart. "Search me, O God, and know my heart; try me, and know my anxieties" (Ps. 139:23 NKJV). The psalmist encourages God to search him out. He wants God to understand how he feels. At times, God is the One who helps us understand how we feel.

6. "You **look deep** within the **mind** and **heart**, O righteous God" (NLT). "How can I know all the **sins lurking** in my **heart**? **Cleanse** me from these **hidden faults** (NLT). "God would surely have **known** it, for he **knows** the **secrets** of every **heart**" (NLT). "O LORD, you have **examined** my **heart** and **know** everything about me" (NLT).

7. "When doubts filled my mind, your comfort gave me renewed hope and cheer" (Ps. 94:19 NLT).

8. "But let a man examine himself, and so let him eat of the bread and drink of the cup" (1 Cor. 11:28 NKJV). Each time we are served Communion in our churches, we are called to examine our hearts. This is just one chance provided for us within the community of Christ.

9. "Examine me, O LORD, and prove me; Try my mind and my heart" (Ps. 26:2 NKJV). God is able to gently convict us of areas that need attention in our hearts. Impure motives. Sins that need uprooting. Attitudes that need adjusting. Wounds that need a healing touch.

10. "Let us search out and examine our ways, And turn back to the LORD" (Lam. 3:40 NKJV). When Jeremiah spoke these words, he was talking to God's people, urging them to see the sin of their ways and turn back to serving the Lord. What I'd like to point out is the connection between examining and turning. Once we know what's in our hearts, and realize that the thing we find there is not right, we must turn to God for help, for forgiveness, for healing. He should always be the One we turn to.

11. "Create in me a clean heart, O God. Renew a right spirit within me" (Ps. 51:10 NLT). God is able to clean us up and renew our spirits. "Restore to me again the joy of your salvation, and make me willing to obey you" (Ps. 51:12 NLT). David asks God to restore him, renew his joy, and to change his attitude. He wants to be willing to obey the Lord.

LESSON 5

1. "Your faith should not be in the wisdom of men but in the power of God" (1 Cor. 2:5 NKJV). Even the wisest of men cannot hope to understand all the ways of God. Paul reminds us not to place our faith in fallible people. Only God is always faithful.

2. "Where is the wise? Where is the scribe? Where is the disputer of this age? Has not God made foolish the wisdom of this world?" (1 Cor. 1:20 NKJV). Find the greatest thinkers, the silver-tongued orators, the most convincing debaters, and the most engaging authors—none of their wisdom can stand up against the wisdom of God. In comparison, they are made to look like fools.

3. "God is wise in heart and mighty in strength. Who has hardened himself against Him and prospered?" (Job 9:4 NKJV). God is wise—alone wise. He knows best, and He's in control. We need to remember that, trust that. If we harden our hearts against Him, how could we possibly expect to prosper?

4. "For the wisdom of this world is foolishness with God. For it is written, 'He catches the wise in their own craftiness'" (1 Cor. 3:19 NKJV). We may try to be wise, but even on our best day, we're hopeless compared to God.

5. "Great is our Lord, and mighty in power; His understanding is infinite" (Ps. 147:5 NKJV). We are finite beings, but God's understanding of everything is infinite. There's nothing He cannot grasp. He understands what makes us tick, what we want and need, and what our limitations are.

6. __b__ , __e__ , __a__ , __c__ , __d__

7. "Shall the **potter** be esteemed as the **clay**; For shall the thing **made** say of him who **made** it, 'He did not **make** me'? Or shall the thing formed say of him who **formed** it, 'He has no **understanding**'?" (Is. 29:16 NKJV). "But now, O LORD, You are our Father; We are the **clay**, and You our **potter**; And all we are the **work** of Your **hand**" (Is. 64:8 NKJV). "But indeed, O man, who are you to reply against God? Will the thing **formed** say to him who **formed** it, '**Why** have you **made** me like this?' Does not the **potter** have **power** over the **clay**?" (Rom. 9:20–21 NKJV)

8. "He will be a vessel for honor, sanctified and useful for the Master, prepared for every good work" (2 Tim. 2:21 NKJV). No matter what shape the Potter has molded us into, if we have the faith to follow His lead, we'll be useful to Him. His craftsmanship has prepared us for the work He's made for us—and it will be a good work.

9. "But as for you, you meant evil against me; but God meant it for good, in order to bring it about as it is this day, to save many people alive" (Gen. 50:20 NKJV). Joseph must have been disappointed by the turn of events his life took. One bad thing came right after the other. At the time he could not have known that his brothers' cruelty was his ticket to the place God needed him. How could he guess that false accusations and prison time would bring him before Pharaoh? And who could've known that one man in the right place at the right time could have brought about the salvation of all his people from starvation and death?

10. "And we **know** that **all things** work together for **good** to those who **love** God, to those who are **called** according to **His purpose**" (Rom. 8:28 NKJV).

11. "Some trust in chariots, and some in horses; But we will remember the name of the LORD our God" (Ps. 20:7 NKJV). Horses and chariots were status symbols in Bible times, and a nation with many of them felt secure from enemy attacks. The king who placed more value in their standing army's abilities than in God's was soon chastised. "It is better to trust in the LORD than to put confidence in man" (Ps. 118:8 NKJV). "He who trusts in his own heart is a fool, but whoever walks wisely will be delivered" (Prov. 28:26 NKJV). We can't see the big picture, and our understanding is so limited. In the end, we can't even trust ourselves.

12. "Those who know Your name will put their trust in You; For You, LORD, have not forsaken those who seek You" (Ps. 9:10 NKJV). We can trust God because He'll never forsake us. "The LORD is my rock and my fortress and my deliverer; My God, my strength, in whom I will trust; My shield and the horn of my salvation, my stronghold" (Ps. 18:2 NKJV). David trusted God because of all the things He was to him—because of all the ways God had proven trustworthy. Look at David's list here—my rock, my fortress, my deliverer, my strength, my shield, my salvation, my stronghold! "You who fear the LORD, trust in the LORD; He is their help and their shield" (Ps. 115:11 NKJV). The psalmist here adds a couple more reasons that God is worthy of our trust. He is our help and our shield.

LESSON 6

1. __b__ , __e__ , __a__ , __c__ , __d__

2. "I, the LORD, search the heart, I test the mind, even to give every man according to his ways, according to the fruit of his doings" (Jer. 17:10 NKJV). God tests our faith and He tests our hearts. He knows the desires, motivations, and intentions hidden in our hearts. When we are put into a crisis, our true metal is revealed.

3. "The LORD your God is testing you to know whether you love the LORD your God with all your heart and with all your soul" (Deut. 13:3 NKJV). We say we have faith and we say we love God, but we are not easily budged out of our comfort zones. Sometimes God's testing is to see how far we will go for love of Him.

4. "I know also, my God, that You **test** the **heart** and have **pleasure** in **uprightness**" (1 Chr. 29:17 NKJV). "The righteous God **tests** the **hearts** and **minds**" (Ps. 7:9 NKJV). "The LORD **tests** the **righteous**" (Ps. 11:5 NKJV). "But, O LORD of hosts, You who **test** the **righteous**, and **see** the **mind** and **heart**" (Jer. 20:12 NKJV). "We speak, not as pleasing men, but God who **tests** our **hearts**" (1 Thess. 2:4 NKJV).

5. "The refining pot is for silver and the furnace for gold, But the LORD tests the hearts" (Prov. 17:3 NKJV). The testing of our hearts is compared often in Scripture to the refining process of precious metals like gold and silver.

6. "I will bring the one-third through the **fire**, will **refine** them as **silver** is **refined**, and **test** them as **gold** is **tested**" (Zech. 13:9 NKJV). "But who can endure the day of His coming? And who can stand when He appears? For He is like a **refiner's fire** and like **launderers' soap**. He will sit as a **refiner** and a **purifier** of **silver**; He will **purify** the sons of Levi, and **purge** them as **gold** and **silver**" (Mal. 3:2–3 NKJV). "For

You, O God, have **tested** us; You have **refined** us as **silver** is **refined**" (Ps. 66:10 NKJV). "Each one's work will become clear; for the Day will declare it, because it will be **revealed** by **fire**; and the **fire** will **test** each one's work, of what sort it is" (1 Cor. 3:13 NKJV).

7. "But He knows the way that I take; When He has tested me, I shall come forth as gold" (Job 23:10 NKJV). In the midst of our trials and testing, we tend to focus on the fire. Job's perspective is different. He doesn't deny the strain of his struggles, but he keeps his eyes on the end, when he'll come forth as gold.

8. "My brethren, count it all joy when you fall into various trials, knowing that the testing of your faith produces patience. But let patience have its perfect work, that you may be perfect and complete, lacking nothing" (James 1:2–4 NKJV). As incongruous as it may seem, James is asking believers to face their trials with joy, knowing that they are a tool of God in their lives.

9. "That the genuineness of your faith, being much more precious than gold that perishes, though it is tested by fire, may be found to praise, honor, and glory at the revelation of Jesus Christ" (1 Pet. 1:7 NKJV). Peter says that genuine faith is more precious than gold, though both are tested by fire. In the end, when our faith shines forth as gold, it will bring praise, honor, and glory to Jesus.

10. "But from there you will seek the LORD your God, and you will find Him if you seek Him with all your heart and with all your soul" (Deut. 4:29 NKJV). "You shall love the LORD your God with all your heart, with all your soul, and with all your strength" (Deut. 6:5 NKJV). Wholehearted pursuit. Complete love and trust. These are essential parts of extraordinary faith.

11. "Abraham Your friend forever" (2 Chr. 20:7 NKJV). "And he was called the friend of God" (James 2:23 NKJV). God wants our hearts. Though He expects our obedience, He wants us to love Him with all we are. Abraham did this, and God called him His friend.

12. "No longer do I call you servants, for a servant does not know what his master is doing; but I have called you friends, for all things that I heard from My Father I have made known to you" (John 15:15 NKJV). Those who love God are commanded to obey Him. That is our role as servants. But Jesus welcomed His followers into a more intimate circle. He called them His friends.

LESSON 7

1. "All we like sheep have gone astray; We have turned, every one, to his own way; And the LORD has laid on Him the iniquity of us all" (Is. 53:6 NKJV). "And they said, 'That is hopeless! So we will walk according to our own plans, and we will every one obey the dictates of his evil heart" (Jer. 18:12 NKJV). "For all people walk each in the name of his god, but we will walk in the name of the LORD our God forever and ever" (Mic. 4:5 NKJV).

2. "And now, Israel, what does the LORD your God **require** of you, but to **fear** the LORD your God, to **walk** in all His **ways** and to **love** Him, to **serve** the LORD your God with all your **heart** and with all your **soul**, and to **keep** the commandments of the LORD and His statutes which I command you today for your **good**?" (Deut. 10:12–13 NKJV)

3. <u>c</u> , <u>h</u> , <u>f</u> , <u>b</u> , <u>g</u> , <u>a</u> , <u>e</u> , <u>d</u>

4. Proverbs 2:7 – Walk **uprightly**. Micah 6:8 – Walk **humbly**. Acts 21:24 – Walk **orderly**. Romans 6:4 – Walk **in newness of life**. Romans 13:13 – Walk **properly**. Galatians 5:25 – Walk **in the Spirit**. Ephesians 5:15 – **Walk circumspectly**.

5. Psalm 26:11 – Walk in **integrity**. Psalm 86:11 – Walk in **Your truth**. Psalm 89:15 – Walk in **the light of Your countenance**. Psalm 119:1 – Walk in **the law of the LORD**. Proverbs 2:20 – Walk in **the way of goodness**. John 8:12 – Walk in **the light of life**. Ephesians 5:2 – Walk in **love**. Colossians 2:6 – Walk in **Him**. 1 John 1:7 – Walk **in the light**.

6. "He who says he abides in Him ought himself also to walk just as He walked" (1 John 2:6 NKJV). When in doubt, follow in Jesus' footsteps. Do what Jesus would do.

7. "For the LORD God is a sun and shield; The LORD will give grace and glory; No good thing will He withhold from those who walk uprightly" (Ps. 84:11 NKJV). God knows those who are His, and He knows our hearts. When we follow after Him, walking in faith, He gives us good things. Mind you, we're not talking cash and valuable prizes here, but good things—love, joy, peace, rest, assurance, and the like.

8. "I, therefore, the prisoner of the Lord, beseech you to **walk worthy** of the **calling** with which you were **called**" (Eph. 4:1 NKJV). "That you may **walk worthy** of the Lord, **fully pleasing** Him, being **fruitful** in every good work and **increasing** in the knowledge of God" (Col. 1:10 NKJV). "That you would **walk worthy** of God who **calls** you into His own kingdom and glory" (1 Thess. 2:12 NKJV).

9. "Without faith it is impossible to please Him, for he who comes to God must believe that He is, and that He is a rewarder of those who diligently seek Him" (Heb. 11:6 NKJV). Faith is a must. Without it, no one can please God.

10. "Cause me to hear Your lovingkindness in the morning, for in You do I trust; Cause me to know the way in which I should walk, for I lift up my soul to You" (Ps. 143:8 NKJV). If we want to walk by faith, to walk worthy of the Lord, then we must turn to Him in order to know the way.

11. "Your ears shall hear a word behind you, saying, 'This is the way, walk in it,' Whenever you turn to the right hand or whenever you turn to the left" (Is. 30:21 NKJV). When we follow after the Lord, He leads us along. We cannot get lost because He is guiding us.

12. "As God has distributed to each one, as the Lord has called each one, so let him walk" (1 Cor. 7:17 NKJV). We are each uniquely gifted, uniquely placed vessels for God's use. As God has blessed you, as He has called you, walk.

LESSON 8

1. "Man shall not live by bread alone; but man lives by every word that proceeds from the mouth of the LORD" (Deut. 8:3 NKJV). Our spiritual needs supercede those of our physical body. They're simply more important. This is a point so basic to faith that Jesus used it to counter the temptations of Satan in the wilderness.

2. "For in it the righteousness of God is revealed from faith to faith; as it is written, 'The just shall live by faith'" (Rom. 1:17 NKJV). In this passage, Paul is quoting from the Old Testament. "Behold the proud, His soul is not upright in him; But the just shall live by his faith" (Hab. 2:4 NKJV).

3. "For in Him we live and move and have our being" (Acts 17:28 NKJV). "For us there is one God...and one Lord Jesus Christ, through whom are all things, and through whom we live" (1 Cor. 8:6 NKJV). "I have been crucified with Christ; it is no longer I who live, but Christ lives in me; and the life which I now live in the flesh I live by faith in the Son of God, who loved me and gave Himself for me" (Gal. 2:20 NKJV). "Your life is hidden with Christ in God" (Col. 3:3 NKJV). "In this the love of God was manifested toward us, that God has sent His only begotten Son into the world, that we might live through Him" (1 John 4:9 NKJV).

4. "He died for all, that those who live should live no longer for themselves, but for Him who died for them and rose again" (2 Cor. 5:15 NKJV). Selfishness is set aside when we no longer live for ourselves. Instead we live for Jesus, who gave up His life so that we could have one.

5. "For those who live according to the flesh set their minds on the things of the flesh, but those who live according to the Spirit, the things of the Spirit" (Rom. 8:5 NKJV). Here is the before and after picture. Before, we lived by the whim of our flesh, basing our decisions on what we felt like doing or having. But now, we live according to the Spirit, and we take God's desires for us into consideration before doing anything. "Who Himself bore our sins in His own body on the tree, that we, having died to sins, might live for righteousness by whose stripes you were healed" (1 Pet. 2:24 NKJV). Peter points out that we now live for righteousness. "That he no longer should live the rest of his time in the flesh for the lusts of men, but for the will of God" (1 Pet. 4:2 NKJV). And later, Peter says that we live for the will of God. We want to do what God wants us to do!

6. "I have **come** that they may have **life**, and that they may have it **more abundantly**" (John 10:10 NKJV). Now to Him who is "able to do exceedingly abundantly above all that we ask or think" (Eph. 3:20 NKJV), is determined that we will have a life characterized by that very abundance.

7. "So then, because you are lukewarm, and neither cold nor hot, I will vomit you out of My mouth" (Rev. 3:16 NKJV). Christ cannot abide the men and women whose response to His call is half-hearted at best. Their apathy leaves a bad taste in His mouth.

8. A wholehearted pursuit of Jesus involves all our passion, all our energy. This is a challenge—a goal we can daily aspire to.

9. Deuteronomy 4:29 – **Seek the** LORD with all your heart. Deuteronomy 6:5 – **Love the** LORD with all your heart. Deuteronomy 10:12 – **Serve the** LORD with all your heart. Deuteronomy 30:2 – **Return to the** LORD with all your heart. Deuteronomy 30:10 – **Turn to the** LORD with all your heart. Proverbs 3:5 – **Trust in the** LORD with all your heart. Jeremiah 29:13 – **Search for the** Lord with all your heart. Zephaniah 3:14 – **Rejoice in the** Lord with all your heart. Acts 8:37 – **Believe in the** Lord with all your heart.

10. "As for me, I will see Your face in righteousness; I shall be satisfied when I awake in Your likeness" (Ps. 17:15 NKJV). "He shall pray to God, and He will delight in him, He shall see His face with joy, For He restores to man His righteousness" (Job 33:26 NKJV). "For now we see in a mirror, dimly, but then face to face. Now I know in part, but then I shall know just as I also am known" (1 Cor. 13:12 NKJV). We walk by faith now, and will continue to do so until we see our Lord face to face.

11. "If indeed you continue in the faith, grounded and steadfast, and are not moved away from the hope of the gospel which you heard" (Col. 1:23 NKJV). We continue in the faith. "Rejoicing to see your good order and the steadfastness of your faith in Christ." (Col. 2:5 NKJV). Our faith is steadfast. "And we desire that each one of you show the same diligence to the full assurance of hope until the end" (Heb. 6:11 NKJV). Our faith is filled with assurance right to the end.

12. "Receiving the end of your faith—the salvation of your souls" (1 Pet. 1:9 NKJV). Salvation. Eternal life. Heaven. Living forever with our Savior. The culmination of a life of faith will be ours when we see our Lord and Savior face to face. That is when faith shall become sight! Amen!

NOTES

NOTES

NOTES

_____

_____

_____

_____

_____

_____

_____

_____

_____

_____

_____

_____

_____

_____

_____

_____

_____

_____

_____

_____

_____

NOTES

NOTES

NOTES

Also available from Sheila Walsh . . .

EXTRAORDINARY
FAITH

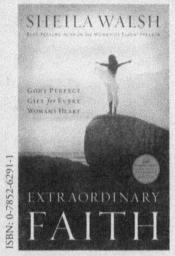

SHEILA WALSH

BEST-SELLING AUTHOR AND WOMEN OF FAITH SPEAKER

GOD'S PERFECT
GIFT for EVERY
WOMAN'S HEART

ISBN: 0-7852-6291-1

EXTRAORDINARY
FAITH

Best-selling author and Women of Faith speaker Sheila Walsh shares insights on the simple, profound, and life-changing gift of faith.

Whether or not you know or even understand it, you are living a life of faith. Perhaps not the conventional, Christian ideal of faith, but faith nonetheless. You flip the light switch and have faith that the light will come on. You turn the key and expect the engine to start. But what about the big things in life? Do you have faith that you'll remain healthy? Faith that your children will be safe from violence? We all face situations that we cannot control. All we can do is trust—and have faith—that God will see us through.

Rather than a complicated, theological enigma, Sheila Walsh explains that faith is a simple, life-giving gift God offers His children. And since it is a gift, He expects us to share it—to give it away. By sharing biblical and modern examples of women of faith, Sheila opens our eyes to the extravagant gift God has for each of us.

NELSON BOOKS
A Division of Thomas Nelson Publishers
Since 1798

www.thomasnelson.com

EXTRAORDINARY*faith*

CONFERENCE 2005

2005 EVENT CITIES & SPECIAL GUESTS

NATIONAL CONFERENCE
LAS VEGAS, NV
FEBRUARY 17-19
Thomas & Mack Center

NATIONAL CONFERENCE
FT. LAUDERDALE, FL
FEBRUARY 24-26
Office Depot Center

SHREVEPORT, LA
APRIL 1-2
CenturyTel Center
*Sandi Patty,
Chonda Pierce,
Jennifer Rothschild*

HOUSTON, TX
APRIL 8-9
Toyota Center
*Kristin Chenoweth,
Natalie Grant,
Jennifer Rothschild*

COLUMBUS, OH
APRIL 15-16
Nationwide Arena
*Avalon,
Kristin Chenoweth,
Nichole Nordeman*

BILLINGS, MT
MAY 13-14
MetraPark
*Sandi Patty,
Chonda Pierce,
Jennifer Rothschild*

PITTSBURGH, PA
MAY 20-21
Mellon Arena
*Natalie Grant,
Nichole Nordeman,
Chonda Pierce*

KANSAS CITY, MO
JUNE 3-4
Kemper Arena
*Natalie Grant,
Chonda Pierce,
Jennifer Rothschild*

ST. LOUIS, MO
JUNE 17-18
Savvis Center
*Avalon,
Nichole Nordeman,
Chonda Pierce*

CANADA & NEW ENGLAND CRUISE
JUNE 25 – JULY 2
Tammy Trent

ATLANTA, GA
JULY 8-9
Philips Arena
*Natalie Grant,
Sherri Shepherd,
Tammy Trent*

FT. WAYNE, IN
JULY 15-16
Allen County War
Memorial Coliseum
*Sandi Patty,
Chonda Pierce,
Jennifer Rothschild*

DETROIT, MI
JULY 22-23
Palace of Auburn Hills
*Sherri Shepherd,
Tammy Trent,
CeCe Winans*

WASHINGTON, DC
JULY 29-30
MCI Center
*Natalie Grant,
Nichole Nordeman,
Sherri Shepherd*

SACRAMENTO, CA
AUGUST 5-6
ARCO Arena
*Avalon,
Kristin Chenoweth,
Tammy Trent*

PORTLAND, OR
AUGUST 12-13
Rose Garden Arena
*Kristin Chenoweth,
Natalie Grant,
Tammy Trent*

DENVER, CO
AUGUST 19-20
Pepsi Center
*Avalon,
Kristin Chenoweth,
Nichole Nordeman*

DALLAS, TX
AUGUST 26-27
American Airlines Center
*Avalon,
Kristin Chenoweth,
Nichole Nordeman*

ANAHEIM, CA
SEPTEMBER 9-10
Arrowhead Pond
*Avalon, Chonda Pierce,
Tammy Trent*

PHILADELPHIA, PA
SEPTEMBER 16-17
Wachovia Center
*Kathie Lee Gifford,
Natalie Grant,
Nichole Nordeman*

ALBANY, NY
SEPTEMBER 23-24
Pepsi Arena
*Sandi Patty,
Chonda Pierce*

HARTFORD, CT
SEPT. 30 – OCT. 1
Hartford Civic Center
*Sandi Patty,
Chonda Pierce,
Tammy Trent*

SEATTLE, WA
OCTOBER 7-8
Key Arena
*Sandi Patty,
Chonda Pierce,
Jennifer Rothschild*

DES MOINES, IA
OCTOBER 14-15
Wells Fargo Arena
*Sandi Patty,
Chonda Pierce,
Jennifer Rothschild*

ST. PAUL, MN
OCTOBER 21-22
Xcel Energy Center
*Sandi Patty,
Chonda Pierce,
Jennifer Rothschild*

CHARLOTTE, NC
OCTOBER 28-29
Charlotte Coliseum
*Sandi Patty, Beth Moore,
Sherri Shepherd*

OKLAHOMA CITY, OK
NOVEMBER 4-5
Ford Center
*Kristin Chenoweth,
Sandi Patty,
Chonda Pierce*

ORLANDO, FL
NOVEMBER 11-12
TD Waterhouse Centre
*Avalon,
Chonda Pierce,
Tammy Trent*

1-888-49-FAITH womenoffaith.com

*Guests subject to change. Not all guests appear in every city. Visit womenoffaith.com for
details on special guests, registration deadlines and pricing.*

WOMEN OF FAITH®